Rebirth from the Ashes

By Allen J. Chinn

Rebirth from the Ashes

The photographs seen in this book are from Allen J. Chinn's personal collection.

ISBN: 978-1-4583-7336-6

PREFACE

All of us have numerous trials in our lives. Life is full of peaks and valleys. We are always on a constant roller coaster ride, sometimes never knowing when we will be upward or downward bound.

Like most people I have had great highs and happiness and yet experienced the gravest of sorrow. We never know how we will deal with these events in our lives.

Sometimes the emotions come from circumstances that we have created. Other times we have no control whatsoever. We must just deal with whatever we are dealt.

I've had an enormous amount of tragedy in my life. I have had six major incidents in the last 21 years. My first divorce, the final departure of my first wife, the passing of my father, my second divorce, the passing of my mother and then betrayal in my 25 year career, were episodes that gave me feelings of deep sadness and loss.

Any of these six major incidents would have been enough to send one into depression.

My bouts with depression have been serious and incapacitating. It had a crippling effect me and changed my daily behavior.

I had various supports that would help break up the compelling feeling of sadness. Unfortunately these short remedies did not have a long term effect.

It wasn't until I sought professional help and made concentrated efforts into the writing and completion of my first book that gave me renewed energy and helped break this cycle of depression.

When I first started working on this book project, I realized that I did not want to write a 300 page detailed account to how I overcame depression or a book of similar magnitude to instruct family and loved ones how to identify and assist someone in recovering from depression.

I know that reading a 300 page book could be a daunting task for most individuals. With depression, it is sometimes difficult just to open mail, let alone attempting to read a large text book.

I decided to write a short memoir describing my personal experience with depression. I was hoping this short, easy to read account of my experiences could help those that were experiencing some degree of depression and also those family and friends that suspect a loved one going through difficulty.

In writing the experiences that lead directly to my depression, I in no way wanted to seem like I was complaining, or attempting to gather sympathy. The events that occurred through my relationships in my marriages and work, and the passing of my parents, were immensely stressful and deeply sad. The brief descriptions in this short memoir are only a tiny fraction of the incidents that happened and a minute indication of the deep sadness I felt.

In many ways this book was very difficult for me to write. I am usually known as a highly skilled and knowledgeable Kung-Fu Great Grandmaster and firearms expert. I am skilled in basketball, volleyball, table tennis and other athletic endeavors. As a recreational professional I was outstanding in the programs I created and the services I provided to the residents of Seattle.

Yet writing this book and retelling my story was very troublesome. In doing so I was admitting to the world I exhibited vulnerability. My strong mind and strong body was not strong enough to cope with the immense sorrow that would eventually become depression.

Though we all have challenges, the way they affect us and how we deal with them, is as different as the individuals experiencing them. This is also true of varying degrees of depression. I hope my brief memoir will help you understand my challenges and the steps I took to be reborn. Hopefully, this book may help you in some positive way.

DEDICATION

To my family and friends that have been my "guardian angels."

To the "walking wounded" and those suffering in silence. May you receive the help you need and be reborn.

To my sons Jason and Brandon, who gave me strength and the reason to carry on.

SPECIAL THANKS

Cori Dang, Melissa Chow, Lynnette Smith and Kathy Chinn for photography.

Melissa Chow for cover design and her original artwork.

Kregg P. J. Jorgenson for his help with reviewing.

TABLE OF CONTENTS

LEGENDS OF THE PHOENIX

The Phoenix is usually known as an ancient mythical symbol of resurrection, rejuvenation and immortality. There are numerous legends from all over the world, regarding this legendary bird.

Cultures of the West, such as Greece, Rome, Egypt and Persia believed the Phoenix to be a legendary bird of fire with bright feathers. The myths surrounding this bird were similar and usually had the bird every 500 (or 1,000) years die, but was magically reborn from its own ashes.

In Chinese mythology, the Phoenix is the symbol of high virtue, grace, power and prosperity.

Unlike the Western Phoenix which goes through a never-ending cycle of birth, death, and rebirth, the Chinese Phoenix is immortal and never dies.

The original name of the Chinese Phoenix is Feng Huang. It incorporates the notions of Feng, a male bird and Huang, a female one, so according to this logic, the bird is actually a symbol of the union between femininity and masculinity, or Yin and Yang.

It is one of the four celestial creatures that the Chinese believed created the world (the other three being the dragon, the unicorn and the tortoise). After the creation of the world, the heavens were divided into four quadrants, one for each creature: north, south, east and west. The Feng Huang ruled over the southern quadrant of heaven, which represented summer and therefore the sun.

The Feng Huang symbolizes justice and graciousness. It does not tolerate lies or the abuse of power, which is why it never appears to people who have low moral standards. The Feng Huang is an extremely kind creature, which is why its legends do not contain any elements of vengefulness; the bird simply shuns away from those who fail to meet its high moral standards.

A common characterization has the Feng Huang attacking snakes with its talons and its wings spread. In fact images of the Feng Huang have appeared in China for over 7000 years.

In artwork where both the Feng Huang and Dragon are together, the Feng Huang symbolized the Empress and the Dragon represented the Emperor. Here the Feng Huang represented power sent from the heavens to the Empress.

If a Feng Huang was used to decorate a house it symbolized that loyalty and honesty were in the people that lived there.

It was also believed that the Feng Huang controlled the 5 tones of Chinese music and that it represented the Confucian virtues.

These classic Confucian virtues are:

Ren. The virtue of benevolence, charity, and humanity.

Yi. The virtue of honesty and uprightness.

Zhong. The virtue of doing one's best, conscientiousness, or loyalty.

Shù. The virtue of reciprocity, altruism, consideration for others, and Confucius' early version of the Golden Rule, "what you don't want yourself, don't do to others."

Li. The virtue of correct behavior, or propriety, good manners, politeness, ceremony, and worship.

The combination of beliefs of what the Phoenix symbolizes for me are: resurrection, rejuvenation, justice and propriety.

LIFE IS YIN AND YANG

Life is the Yin and Yang. For every space of Yin there is an equal amount of space occupied by Yang. These two complimentary forces create the balance in all things. What appear to be contrary elements are actually complimentary. One cannot exist without the other.

My life has been filled with so much positive, but it seemed that greater amounts of negative had taken place. At times it seemed like the bad times would never end.

Perhaps everything is timing. I feel possibly in our life there are times of good, later to be balanced by the bad. Maybe our lives are not rhythmic patterns of good and bad. Conceivably we could have many years of hardship to be later balanced with happiness at a later time.

If we follow the philosophy of Yin and Yang, over our entire lifetime we will experience the balance of good and bad.

THE DEVASTATION OF DIVORCE

I met my first wife on a blind date in July of 1978. I was too young and really didn't understand the vast differences that my future wife and I had. I was open minded, idealistic and believed that if we loved each other, things would work out fine. I was always the romantic type and did everything with my heart and my mind.

I did not understand the ramifications of being with someone that was my opposite in almost every area of life. I was conservative, close to my family, an outdoors sportsman, athletic, and did not smoke. She was my opposite.

I believed in the Yin and Yang philosophy. That what appears as opposites, act as complimentary forces and a balance will exist. However, this philosophy would only work if the two individuals are genuinely working together towards a common goal (relationship, marriage, etc...).

I was like a moth attracted to this very different flame. I had never gone out with anyone like her before. It was a whirlwind romance that led me to ask her to marry me just five months after our blind date.

It was the Christmas of 1978. I had 12 small Christmas gifts wrapped under the tree. She was very surprised by all these gifts. Opening them one at a time as I handed them to her, she was surprised by the diamond ring in the eleventh box. Everything seemed to go well and we were engaged.

I put a down payment on a little house in Kent, Washington and we were going to move in together. She had the experience of living on her own, and I had never been anywhere except living with my parents.

Her conditions for moving in with me were simple. She said she would not move into the house until there was a refrigerator and television there. I worked in Auburn at the time. One day I purchased a refrigerator and television at lunch time and dropped it off to the house. I had a friend with a pickup truck and he helped me move the big refrigerator. I put a bottle of champagne and glasses in it to be chilled.

After work, I drove back to Seattle to pick her up and suggested that we should take a look at the house in Kent. We went to the cute little rambler and I surprised her. We moved in together soon after.

I remember a few months before my wedding; my father stopped me and wanted to talk to me. He asked me if I really wanted to get married. I stated "Yes." He then in his "Archie Bunker type" old school logic said, "If you're getting the milk, why buy the cow?"

I was incensed by this remark. I loved her and because I loved her, we were going to be married. Thirteen months after that first date, we were married.

On my wedding day, everything seemed to be going fine, yet there were all these omens that I didn't recognize at the time. She and I drove together, but were running late. Being late was always one of her traits. When we arrived at the church, she was nervous and needed a shot of alcohol. My father and mother got into a fight. My sister Susan and her husband Wally got into a fight. Her two sisters got into fights with their husbands.

Our wedding planner sent me and the groomsmen down the back hallway late. When walking in the dark back hallway, I tripped over a heavy metal obstacle left in the middle of the floor. I caught my balance, but there was a large black scuff mark left from the impact from the heavy object.

By the time we reached the altar, three of the bridesmaids were already walking down the aisle.

This continual flow of bad luck and bad omens did not stop there. When we arrived at the wedding banquet, we thought everything was going as planned. We did not know that the menu was changed by the restaurant and lesser quality food was served to our guests.

Was a higher power trying to warn me?

Within a short time I was full of doubt and uncertainty about my marriage. I had an unloving relationship and it seemed that my wife never appreciated me and didn't return my love and affection.

She could not say the words "I love you." She could say these three words to her cats, but not to me. This fact added to my growing insecurity. I always felt an impending doom, as I felt my wife was always looking for "greener pastures." I always felt that I would be replaced and that my love for her was never good enough.

After a year of marriage we had our first son, Jason. A few months after his birth we went to a marriage counselor. This proved to be useless.

After our initial meeting and questioners, the counselor stated that I was happy, positive, optimistic and had high self esteem. He stated that my wife was unhappy with herself, pessimistic and had low self esteem. He stated that I would not be going to anymore sessions and he would be concentrating on her.

We came to him seeking help with our marriage, but now he was only going to work with one of us. This was insane. There was no interaction, or working together because of this strange direction.

Going to him was like seeing a car mechanic, only to have him state the obvious. Then work on part of the problem, but not work to repair what was needed in the first place. Seeing this counselor was not productive.

I once asked her: "Why did you marry me?" Her reply was: "Nothing else was going on at the time." That hurt and I certainly felt belittled.

Another time I asked her: "Do you love me?" Her response was: "I don't think I ever loved you." Again, I was devastated with her callous reply.

My heart felt like there was an open wound. For all my pain, I still loved her. She had this "lock" on my heart. I always loved her and my children. This situation would remain the same for years.

In 1988, our marriage was still stressful. She started volunteering at church during week nights, when she should have been home with the children. I always uneasy about this. I believe she was interested in someone at church and that compelled her to volunteer more.

By 1989 I had had enough. I continued to feel worthless in this marriage and knew that it was always just a matter of time before I was replaced. After years of feeling this way, I knew whatever sparkle appeared in her eyes, were not because of me.

Though I still loved her, I knew this marriage was pointless. No matter what I did, she would never love me.

The divorce would be devastating. It has been stated that a divorce is as stressful and painful, as if there was a death of a close family member. It was.

I tried to get through this divorce with minimal complications and animosity. I discussed this with her and we decided to use Washington Dissolution Service. It was a divorce service for uncontested divorces.

I remember meeting her downtown to sign the papers. I still felt uneasy about this situation. I knew that the life I had with her and my children would be forever changed. I could not continue this life of uncertainty and have a life partner that did not love me.

We signed the papers. The process went by smoothly and quickly. As we left the office we paused outside the building. We said good bye and she left to go back to her office. As she turned and walked away, I felt sadness and a part of me was gone. I walked to my car a couple of blocks away and also went back to work.

A week or so went by and then she had changed her mind. Her friends informed her that she should hold out for more. That is exactly what she did. She hired an attorney and now she wanted to go to court.

Whatever had been agreed to in previous conversations was now out the window. She had stated when we were in the first house, that she would never take my house away from me if we were ever to break up. Prior to going to Washington Dissolution Service, we agreed that I would borrow $9,000.00 to pay off her credit card bills and I could keep the house. I wanted the house to be one stable thing in our children's life.

Now we were going down a road where disagreements and animosity would be rampant. She was now Kathleen Turner and I was Michael Douglas in "War of the Roses." What started out with romance, slowly over years became discontentment and unhappiness. Now with a battle ready to take place in court, it was turning very ugly.

To add to the great stress and mixed emotions, she and I stayed in the same house. We even stayed in the same bed! Crazy! Neither one of us wanted to move out to give the other an advantage in court.

On one occasion, I drove up to Vancouver B.C. I decided that it would be good for me to get out of town and visit my friends Ken Low and Neil Chan. They were my closest friends in Canada.

I never liked doing things on my own. Especially long drives. I was very sad as I drove up towards the Canadian border. I felt like my morning was a collision of all my feelings of loss and remorse. It was so emotional and driving was difficult. Then I placed a tape of Eddie Murphy's Raw in my player.

I knew that his live comedy performance would keep me laughing. A large part of his stand-up routine was devoted to divorce. He started with comments about his girlfriend and how he wasn't going to marry her. Then he mentioned Johnny Carson and his wife in a 50 million dollar law suit.

He later said he was going to marry some African woman from the bush, buck-ass naked, riding a zebra with a bone in her hair. This tape lifted my spirit and made me laugh about divorce. Misery loves company and I was able to laugh at the animated situations that made my own look insignificant.

This comedy tape saved my visit to my dear friends up North. Instead of arriving emotional and shaky, I was energized and temporarily didn't think about my troubles back home.

Once I got home, my situation continued to be so stressful and so crazy!!! I was still in love with this woman that had a lock on my heart, while she seemed callous and uncaring as she was taking my life away from me. She seemed quite emotionless throughout the process.

It was driving me to insanity! She would state that she was told by her friends that she could have this and that. I would even call her attorney to clarify things my wife was asking about. I was on the brink of insanity.

One day my niece Cori gave me Madonna's single CD "Take a Bow." She was only about 10 years old at the time. I was touched how she was so sweet and thoughtful. Cori selected a song with lyrics that fit my situation perfectly. Just like the song, I was always in love with her, and she knew it was true. Also like the song she took my love for granted and it was finally over.

She wrote a nice note on a little yellow "post it" stating that things would be better for me and I deserved happiness. Whenever I hear this song I think about the lyrics, the "post it" note and the thoughtfulness of my young 10 year old niece.

I overheard my wife one day stating that one of her friends said that she could have over $800.00 a month in child support. That was the last straw! I knew I was the better parent. I had the patience and ability to work with my children through all their homework challenges. I was there to support them through all of their special needs and be the strong foundation that they needed.

I went to her and stated that I should sue her for custody of the children. I said I was the better parent. I had a proven track record of a stable family background and my work was with children and families.

I said that this situation was crazy! The only ones making out of this divorce would be the attorneys. The more we fought, the more the attorneys made. That would mean less for us to restart our lives, and less for the children.

She listened to my reasoning and we agreed on joint custody of the children and the property was divided equally in value. We met with the attorneys and all four of us signed the legal documents.

Then we waited for the divorce to be finalized. More stress and the waiting was grueling. Just like the movie "War of the Roses!" Both combatants unwilling to move out. Luckily we didn't go to the extremes of poisoning food, or suffocation with pillows.

Finally the divorce was final and the day that I never wanted to happen was there. We were now exes.

Our plans were just as different as our personalities had been. My direction was to keep the house and make it seem less of a change for our sons Jason and Brandon.

Her plans were to buy a condo and restart her life as soon as possible.

I remember the great difficulty I had when her friends came over to the house to help her pack up her things and furniture. I thought I was in control of my emotions, but I felt pain and loss as her friends were wrapping up dishes and carrying out furniture.

This was no longer academic, this was reality. And the reality was that the person that I loved, cherished, planned our future together with, married, defended, argued with, and fought with, was no longer going to be a part of my life.

The life I knew for the last 10 years would never be the same again.

All my hopes and dreams of growing old together would disappear. Yet everything that we purchased together and everything we did together would have haunting memories for me.

From the microwave I purchased for her celebrating our one month anniversary; the rocking chair that I purchased for her before our first son was born; the refrigerator that she shot; everything had a memory associated with her.

Even the house had our unique history. In 1982 we purchased the house on contingency that our first house would sell. We picked the colors, the cabinets, the carpet; I even had to have a brick chimney. We went to the plot often and took pictures of the foundation being put in, the walls and the construction.

In 1982 the housing market was not doing very well at the time and our home did not sell. We stayed in that first home for another three years. She was pressuring me to buy another home as our family numbered four then. I wasn't impressed with the areas she wanted to move to, so I suggested that we should look in the area that we had that house built three years earlier.

We drove to the community and to our great surprise, the house was for sale. We stopped and knocked on the door and a woman answered stating it was just placed on the market that morning. Her family had been renting from the owner. The woman was kind enough to let us in and we saw that nothing had changed since we built it.

We immediately contacted our real estate agent and told her about the history of the house we had built three years earlier. It was our "dream house."

She contacted the agent representing the owner and found out her history. The woman and her husband purchased the new house a year after we had it built. Before they could move in, the husband ran off with another woman. The wife kept the house, but could not bear to stay in the bedroom and chose to stay in the family room. She had been renting out the house and now that she was going to remarry, there was no need to keep it.

Our real estate agent told the other agent and the owner our story. The owner was so moved by our story she decided accept our offer, even though it was a seller's market at the time. By the end of the day the house was ours.

This house had so many memories in the next four years. All our family celebrations and parties, our Christmases, everything was locked here.

This was the house that I wanted to keep after the divorce.

PROLONGING THE INEVITABLE

Life has many twists and no one can imagine the strange occurrences that can take place.

This was just another difficult time for us. Dealing with the creation of two separate households, getting a schedule coordinated to shuttle the children back in forth and trying to become "single" again were challenges.

My ex-wife had purchased a condo about 20 minutes away from what was our house. She purchased her home nearby so the children would be at the same school and transportation would be an easy chore for the both of us.

She wanted everything new. Except for some furniture, dishes, pictures, and appliances, she went and purchased the rest. She didn't have the ability to set up her electronics, so I went over to help her put together her stereo equipment and televisions.

She purchased new Dania furniture for herself and the children. Here I was helping her again with the assembly of furniture. She was never very adept at assembly furniture, or similar objects.

We had keys to each other's house. Since we were transporting the children back in forth each week, we found it simpler to permit our "ex" to bring them into the house and not have to wait in the car if one of us was late.

Though this was nice for ex-spouses to permit, this creates issues in other areas. I remember I had called and was trying to set up a date with a woman I had met at martial arts tournaments. I wondered why she had not called back after our last conversation.

I called her and she said that she had been really busy. She thought that "it" probably wouldn't work out with us. Then she stated that she actually did call, but a woman answered the phone. She must have thought the worst of me. I explained that only could have been my ex-wife and she was probably dropping off the children. She accepted the explanation and said maybe it could work out.

I never did call her back. I hesitated as I was no longer any good at being "single." Being a single parent is tough regardless of gender. This is especially true with very active children.

My ex-wife and I found out that it was an easier to be together than apart. For the children it seemed more like we were a family again and for us there was support for each other. I was the support person that could deal with the children's homework, provide discipline and fix things as needed.

She provided the companionship that I needed. In my heart I still loved her.

More and more we were finding that we needed each other and we spent more time together. We started acting like a couple again and we found each other spending the night where the children were scheduled to be at.

These strange incidents continued and soon she moved back into our house. She rented out her condo. We created a strange relationship and confused all of our family and friends.

This was not an easy relationship for either of us. She did not love me, or respect me the same way I felt for her. There were times of stress and she had moved out two or three times, only to move back together with me.

We took a family vacation to Hawaii in 1998. My sister's family and our family took this summer trip together. A couple of days into the trip I found a spot for dinner on the Kona beach. I thought it would be nice to have a romantic dinner without our sons and see the Hawaiian sunset together. My sister and brother-in-law took the boys for that evening.

As my ex-wife and I were getting our dinner, I mentioned that I just took a great workshop. We both worked for the City of Seattle and she asked what the workshop about. I said that it was about communication. The premise was different types of people and personalities would communicate in a specific way. It would be important to understand how the different personalities communicate, in order to facilitate better communication with them.

I said that the different personalities were divided up into four color groups. She said that she had taken that very same workshop and thought it was good. She then asked me what colors I said that related to me.

I said that I was blue and red. She immediately said, "I don't see that." I asked her, "What colors do you think I am?" She said, "I think you're green and brown." I was surprised and shocked and asked her what colors she said she was. She said that she had felt she was blue and red.

In the workshop the color blue indicated a person that communicated with emotion and feeling. The color red was about fun and creativity, brown was direct and green was one that needed numbers and statistics to communicate.

This started off a huge fight and the evening was ruined. What the workshop failed to instill in us, was that how we see ourselves can be different from how others see us. Also, we may communicate with some people in one manner and others in a different way.

We would make up as we had done numerous times before. Though the relationship seemed to be mended, we were still not a good match. In my heart I loved her, but she did not love me. It appeared that the situation was better dealt with as a couple. Unfortunately we were not a real couple.

It would appear that unrequited love would be my destiny with this woman. Convenience would be her reason to be with me.

DEPRESSION

In 2000, my ex-wife and I were continuing our strange relationship. I remember one evening I asked if she was coming over the next day. She said she couldn't. I asked why and after a moment of hesitation, she admitted that she was seeing someone. I couldn't believe this. It seemed like things were going well between us.

What I had imagined all those years finally happened. I was just there to fill in the time until she found someone better.

She packed up her things and moved back to her condo. It was finally over.

I felt a great loss again. We had this long 10 year relationship after our divorce. This too finally had come to an end.

A short time passed and then I started experiencing things that I had never had before. I lost joy in doing things that I usually liked. I didn't want to go out. I tried to appear "normal" to my children, family, friends and co-workers.

I was usually "clock watcher" and didn't appreciate those that didn't make the effort to be on time. I have had people in my life that were chronically late. They did not respect the people that were waiting for them. They were too self centered and felt that they were more important than the people that made the effort to be on time. I almost always arrived early to ensure being late was not an option. I led by example.

One of the strange symptoms was my inability to get out of bed. I would set my alarm two hours before my start time at Queen Anne Community Center. This would give me an hour to get ready and an hour for the long 22 mile commute through the back roads of Renton, the I-5 freeway, downtown Seattle and finally up Queen Anne Hill.

My alarm would go off, I would be awake, but I could not leave my bed. I would lie, or sit there, under my sheets, but could not move. Thoughts would race through my head, but my body appeared to have no energy to move.

The time would go down to one hour before my start time, and I still could not move. At 45 minutes to start time, suddenly the continued realization that I would be late would give me just enough energy to force myself out of bed. Then I would race like a madman cleaning up, and speeding through traffic. I would make it work, but felt bad because I would be 10 to 15 minutes late.

This situation bothered me, but it became a daily ritual. I could not get the energy to move until I knew I was going to be late. Each day only the realization that I was going to be late, got my body to move into "emergency mode." It was the only way to get my butt moving.

On the weekends it was worse. I would wake up only to stay in bed all day. I would get up to eat, or use the bathroom, but I would find myself back in the safe, warm bed all weekend. I would watch television from the bed and that was all I needed, or wanted to do.

On Monday morning the fight to get out of bed and get to work on time would start all over again. These symptoms and the desire not to be late created more stress for me.

I have had periods of sadness, but the "blues" were nothing like what I was experiencing.

No one knew of my condition. I was normally an energetic, positive, happy person. Yet at this time it was a mask, hiding my grief and sadness. Like most people, I did not want anyone to know what I was going through.

I had joined the "walking wounded." I was depressed and though I looked physically fine, I was indeed "injured." My mind and heart suffered a great loss. I could not control how, or what I was feeling.

Though I knew that I should be able to do the things I enjoyed and it should be an easy task to just get up out of bed, my mind could not control my body to do these simple acts. I was powerless.

Finally I asked a co-worker one day if they had ever gone to a therapist before. At first this co-worker was a little hesitant. Maybe a little defensive also. They may have thought I was suggesting for them to go see one. When they found out the inquiry was for me, they opened up and said it was a great experience for them. "It was like talking to a friend, but you can say everything and be open. It was refreshing."

With that answer I knew it was time for me to see a therapist for help. I knew I needed the help to get well. I knew I had to be back to my old self to be the best I could be for my sons.

I contacted our Employee Assistant Program and they referred me to a therapist in Northgate.

HELPED BY AN ANGEL

This whole situation with depression was very strange to me. I was physically strong and healthy, but depression had crippled me. My strong Kung-Fu background gave me a strong mind and will, but depression was a very different beast.

I researched depression and found out that I had joined the estimated 18 million Americans that suffer from it. Approximately 9 million Americans have major or clinical depression. Alarmingly, two-thirds of people suffering from depression do not seek the necessary treatment.

Furthermore, this serious condition cost Americans an estimated $26 billion that year. The effects of this serious condition can cripple the individual. The long term effects on relationships and families are unimaginable.

I went to my first appointment to meet this therapist, not knowing what to expect.

I found the office and went in. I sat in the lobby area until I was greeted. A tall, slender woman appeared. She was dressed in what looked like "hippie" tie dye clothing that I remembered from the 1970s. Her name was Lynn.

When meeting her, I did not realize that this would be the person that would be able to help me.

She was friendly and listened well. She did not direct our conversations, well at least not overtly. It was easy to talk to her and I felt comfortable with her.

I believe it was my second visit when I asked if all my symptoms were due to my ex-wife. She responded with, "Of course not. Not the woman that you spent the last 20 years with and not the mother of your children." Yes, I figured she was being sarcastic. Her easy going manner and soft tone, kept it funny for me. I smiled and laughed.

She said that we had four more sessions to work through the issues. She also said that if I wanted to pursue any medication I would have to have my doctor prescribe them to me, as she could not do that.

In the next four sessions Lynn made me realize that I was going through a grief process. The woman that I loved for the last 20 years was no longer there. It was that realization that created my symptoms.

Lynn helped me acknowledge the grief I was feeling and my own medical doctor prescribed the Prozac for me. I was feeling better about the loss of my ex-wife. Unfortunately the Prozac caused "ringing of the ears" and I could hear a high pitched sound constantly.

I tried different medications in Zoloft and Paxil. Though I no longer lingered in bed in the mornings, I could not get rid of the "ringing of the ears."

I was thankful to Lynn for her help in opening my eyes to what was causing all these issues. I was happy that my employer had the Employee Assistance Program for me to take advantage of.

RELENTLESS WAVES OF STRESS AND SADNESS

In the summer of 2000 I met another woman destined to be a future ex-wife. She too was a blind date.

I soon fell in love with her, but fell into a cyclic "on and off again" relationship. Of course this lead to more and greater stress.

Though we loved each other, it became apparent to me that she was listening to her family and friends. Whatever I had to say seemed important, but not as important as the words coming from those that she felt she could trust more.

I was not Korean, and not many things that seemed important to her. She knew I was a great father and soon became a father and advocate for her two daughters. She knew that I truly loved her, but that was not enough.

My father had been ill for some time and his reduced activities weakened his once strong body. Things started to go downhill once he had his stroke in 1985. He no longer was the strong, fast Kung-Fu Master that had fingers of steel and a lightning fast lotus kick. He no longer was the great outdoorsman that could hunt the fields all day and stay out on the lakes from sunrise to sundown.

During our trip to Hong Kong in 1997, he had great difficulty walking three city blocks. Though he was 79 years old at the time, he insisted to make it to the various stores to buy gifts to bring home to his family.

My father had developed diabetes and had high blood pressure. Other than these conditions his health was fine for a man his age.

He started to go to the hospital increasingly because all his organs slowly stopped functioning correctly.

My sister Susan took him to most of his appointments. My brother Steve and I took him to appointments when we could. My father had several emergency visits to the hospital. We would all go to visit him at the nursing homes that he was sent to.

I remember I drove my mother to visit him at the nursing home at Mercer Island. As we showed up, my father was sitting in a wheel chair, dressed in his street clothes. As my mother and I greeted him, he told us that the nursing staff said he was fine and he could go home. I knew this sounded a little funny. I asked him to wait a minute for me to check it out. He assured me it was fine for him to leave.

I checked with the staff and went back to my father. I told him that didn't know anything about him leaving, and I wheeled him back to his room. He was just trying to pull a "fast one." No one could blame him. He didn't like the food and just wanted to be home.

In time he worsened. He made several trips to Swedish Hospital, but during his last visit he did not get better. He was hooked up to a respirator, but lost the ability to communicate. We visited at different times. I remembered that at first contact he would recognize us and smile. Then in just a few minutes he would lay in the hospital bed, unresponsive.

We tried keeping my father alive as long as possible, but his health could not improve. My father passed away in January of 2004.

It was hard dealing with his passing. Right after his funeral my mother wanted me to stay with her, and I spent the night on the sofa. We followed Chinese tradition and left the porch light on so my father's spirit could find his way home.

My father had a huge effect on shaping me. It was his inspiration that I became a Kung-Fu master, shot competitively, and enjoyed working in the outdoor sporting goods and firearms industry. He taught me table tennis and his old school logic was priceless. He was a man's man, multi-talented and tough when he needed to be. I miss him greatly.

My mother tried staying in the house, but it was just too much for her. My sister and brother-in-law found a home near them and remodeled it for her. We cleaned the house and moved her to the new home in Bellevue. She seemed quite happy there. Thanks to Susan and Wally, she lived comfortably and very close to them. They were able to respond to her emergencies quickly as she was only 10 minutes away.

I got married in the summer of 2004. The on and off again relationship with my Korean girlfriend seemed to be stable and I had been a good father to her daughters. I took them to school every day, helped them with their studies and went to all the teacher/parent conferences. We played basketball, video games and watched our movies together. I also taught them Kung-Fu.

Things seemed to go well for over a year, so we got married in July. We actually had to postpone our wedding and honeymoon by one week to accommodate opening the new International District/Chinatown Community Center. I was given a month and a half to furnish, create programs and special events, produce a brochure and open the facility to the public.

I worked alone on this assignment and accomplished it successfully. The new facility was a hit with the community. There was new found pride in this community center from both the community and the department. Unfortunately with all the stress that this monumental task created for me, I suffered neck and shoulder pain for the next six months.

My marriage was not as stable as I had hoped. There was a still a cultural and communication gap with my wife. She still trusted her family and her Korean friends more than me.

The turning point in our marriage was when I sold my house in Renton. The escrow company I was using said it was important to have my current wife sign an agreement that she had no interest in the house, since I owned the house prior to our marriage.

I let my second wife know that this was important in order to sell and close the house. She agreed to meet me at the escrow agent's office at 3:00 p.m. She never showed up. The escrow agent contacted their manager and though they would have preferred to have a statement releasing all interest of the property from my second wife, they proceeded to close the property anyway.

I'm sure her family and friends told her not to show up and sign the release. This led to increased problems and our relationship was never the same. We were divorced months later.

My mother was ill. She didn't want surgery because of her advanced age. She and her doctors knew that a person in their 80s would have a great difficulty recovering from a major surgery.

She started dialysis treatment at the Northwest Kidney Centers. Susan and Wally were spending so much time taking her; Steven and I jumped in and divided up the weekly trips to the treatments.

My mother was starting to get weak and sometimes fell. Eventually Susan, Wally, Steven and I would take shifts staying at her house to ensure her safety and comfort.

We started to do the dialysis in home with a dialysis machine. We all learned the proper procedures and how to use the machine. This was just another thing that we had to do to keep her going.

Due to her declining health, I filed Family Medical Leave papers with my Department. This permitted me to take time off to take care of her. Sometimes I used the leave to take her to doctor's appointments. Other times I had extended periods that I needed to provide care for her.

My usual shift was Monday through Thursday evenings. I would arrive immediately after work and spend the night. Susan would come in the morning to relieve me so I could go home to shower and change for work.

I spent many nights in the hospital with my mother. In fact she and I spent the night in the hospital just before my niece Melissa's wedding in 2007. We rushed back to her home and rushed around getting her ready. She really wanted to be at her granddaughter's wedding.

Like my father, she got increasingly weaker. Sadly, she started to go to the emergency room more often. We continued our shifts, whether they were at her home, or at the hospital. She would be incoherent at times and then the frequency increased.

The last time she was admitted into the Emergency Room at Swedish Hospital, was unforgettable. My mother was taken off the medication to keep her "merely alive" and was now given medication to make her feel more comfortable. The hospice process had been started.

At 3 a.m. she was calling for Susan. In a loud voice she called "Gehyan-ah, Gehyan-ah!" This was my sister's Chinese name. She did this about four times. I told her Susan was at home sleeping. She told me that she needed Susan's help to organize a trip to San Francisco with Cheng Seim (her friend since childhood). I smiled as this was strange. I couldn't remember my mother ever visiting San Francisco. In my heart I was sad as I knew she was delirious and the end was near.

Steven was at the hospital with her that weekend. I brought my second ex-wife to visit. My mother's eyes lit up when she saw her. They always had a good relationship and my mother was always fond of her. They held hands for a moment, then my mother repeated "bye bye" several times. My second ex-wife and I looked at each other as this was a little odd. But knowing her condition, we understood.

My mother passed away two days later. This was in February of 2008. Her death was hard to deal with. I was extremely close to her. As a child she was the parent that we had most contact with. She worked day shifts and was able to be there for us in the evening. She made all our meals for us every day, enforced all the rules of the home and dealt out almost all the discipline.

She taught us unconditional love, self-sacrifice and how to worry. I have so many memories and I especially treasure my mother's teaching moments. It seems that most of my memories were of her teaching moments, because she lived every day the way we should and led by example.

THE KNOCKOUT BLOW

I was blindsided by a coworker. This individual collaborated with a friend and created numerous false complaints about me.

This friend filed complaints against me, stating that I was a racist and I was violating city, state and federal safety rules. The Department and the Superintendent did the worse damage. Instead promptly researching the initial complaint without bias and doing a comprehensive check on my background, the new Superintendent interjected and had me immediately placed on administrative reassignment.

I was placed on administrative reassignment to our South Lake Union facility. I was thoroughly embarrassed and everyone knew something was not quite right. "Why would Allen be down here instead of running his community center?" I felt everyone was thinking this and their suspicions were correct.

Several people I knew gave me puzzled looks when they found out I was temporarily relocated there. It was like the captain of a star ship working out of an office on some obscure planet. You and everyone else would know that you should be running the ship!

I kept checking with our Human Resource Office, trying to find a way to expedite the situation. They seemed to drag their feet. Finally they stated only they Superintendent could take me off administrative reassignment, because he was the one that placed me on administrative reassignment. Though I was found not guilty of any of these charges, I remained at the South Lake Union facility for a total of five weeks.

I was under so much stress and sadness. I had lost my father in 2004, been through a second divorce in 2005, had been taking care of my ailing mother in 2007, and finally lost her just two months before all the Department issues came up from the false allegations.

All of the false complaints and actions against me ended up giving me anxiety and depression. After all my grief and suffering, I now had to deal with a coworker that I thought I knew and trusted, and a Department that I worked for 25 years, treating me like a stranger and criminal.

I choose to use my annual Employee's Assistance Program allotted hours and visit a therapist. I was also going through so much stress with the death of my mother. I requested a therapist near my home. The Employee's Assistance Program gave me the name of a therapist within two miles from my home.

When I first met Dora, she was very easy going and somehow I felt comfortable like I was talking with an aunt. We spoke for a while and she got to know about my background and why I was there to see her.

I had mentioned going through my second divorce and the passing of my mother. My issues at work were brought up. I even mentioned I was saddened by the loss of the Seattle SuperSonics and their move to Oklahoma.

At first Dora decided to work with me on my grief and loss issues. She explained to me that we all experience grief. Dora stated that even if we lost a wallet, some grief would be experienced. She worked with me on the five stages of grief.

Denial. At first, we tend to deny the loss has taken place, and may withdraw from our usual social contacts. This stage may vary in its length.

Anger. The grieving person may then be furious at the person who inflicted the hurt (even if they are dead), or at the world, for letting it happen. They may be angry at them self for letting the event take place, even if, realistically, nothing could have stopped it.

Bargaining. Now the grieving person may make bargains with God, asking, "If I do this, will you take away the loss?"

Depression. The grieving person feels numb, although anger and sadness may remain underneath.

Acceptance. This is when the anger, sadness and mourning have tapered off. The person simply accepts the reality of the loss.

These five stages, denial, anger, bargaining, depression and acceptance are a guide for learning to live with the one we lost. They are just tools to help us identify what we may be feeling. However, these stages are not engraved in stone. Not everyone goes through all of them, or in the suggested order. How each of us deals with grief and loss is as different as the individuals that are experiencing it.

Dora asked me what stage I was in. I told her that I felt that I was in between depression and acceptance. I had accepted the passing of my mother. I just still had some sadness because she was gone.

In the back of my mind, I still felt some guilt and wished that I could have spent even more time with her the years she was healthy. I still felt this way even though we were very close and I was present much of the time.

Later she focused on my relationships. It must have been due to our preliminary conversation. She asked me several questions about what I was looking for in a relationship. She then handed me a form that I needed to complete. On this form it had numerous fields that I would give a numeric score, regarding facets of my relationships. I would fill out all these fields for each of my significant relationships.

When Dora first looked at the completed form she said, "None of these scores are very high." She paused, then peering over her glasses and said, "I bet you they were all pretty weren't they?" I was speechless and a small smile appeared on my face. I was caught.

Dora addressed the fact that I had gone back to my ex-wives, even after break ups and divorce. She said, "Going back to an old relationship is like digging up something that was dead. It is just not the same anymore. Better to leave it buried." I immediately pictured scenes from the movie "Pet Cemetery!"

She was very nice and remarked that I was handsome, intelligent, warm and caring. She thought that it should be very easy to meet a woman that would want a man with all these traits.

Dora appeared to be concerned with my selection process and thought that I should use compatibility factors to make better partner decisions in the future. She mentioned that several of her clients had used an online dating service that was based on compatibility and they were very satisfied with it. I smiled and told her that I was going to take things a little slower for a while.

DEPRESSION AND ANXIETY

With the increased pressure from the coworker continually making false accusations (weekly was the word used by Human Resources), I felt more anxiety. The stress was horrible. I again started feeling depressed.

Within four years I had gone through the deaths of both my parents and my second divorce. I had anxiety and depression. I needed to file the papers to use the Family Medical Leave benefit for my own serious health issue. Sometimes I worked a few days and then I had to take a couple days off. I did this just to recuperate from all the stress that was giving me more anxiety and making me more depressed.

I felt betrayed by the coworker that I mentored and helped.

I felt betrayed by the Department that I worked so hard for. It seemed that the last two and a half decades of service and dedication meant nothing to them.

I was transferred to Miller Community Center. This was a problem for me, as the community center had become something totally different from the philosophy of the "how and why" of community centers being built in the various communities.

My personal feeling was that this facility no longer served the immediate neighborhood. It had become a rental facility more concerned with rental income than servicing the local residents.

This situation was unbearable as this attacked my core values.

FORCED RETIREMENT

I waited for January 1, 2009 to arrive, so I could use the Employee Assistance Program again. My six visits permitted each year would restart at the beginning of the calendar year.

I made an appointment with Dora again. I explained all the new issues with the complaints and scam the co-worker and his friend was doing. She understood what they were trying to pull, but she knew that my supervisors were not supportive and did not make good decisions in this matter.

Dora asked, "Is there any you can do? Find a different job maybe?" I responded, "I guess I could retire." Dora then said, "Well what are you waiting for?"

When the stress of going to work becomes insurmountable, this too becomes a time when we must assess the "relationship." Is the pay still worth the stress and the way you are treated? Do you have your dignity intact? Or have you compromised yourself to the point where you are not valued at all?

What was an easy decision in my heart was a difficult decision financially. I had just turned 52 years old and could qualify for retirement. However, I would only receive 38% of my salary if I retired with 25 years of service. If I could hold out another five years, I could receive 60% of my salary.

After some soul searching it was an easy decision. I knew I needed to leave this job. I was no longer happy with the Department. I knew that poor decisions would be made by my superiors and after all the stress and grief I had experienced personally, they did not care.

I was going through anxiety and depression, but I could clearly see that losing 62% of my salary was worth leaving the lunacy I was being put through.

I felt I was forced to retire through coercion. Coercion is defined as the practice of forcing another party to behave in an involuntary manner (whether through action or inaction). This could be done by use of threats, intimidation or some other form of pressure or force. These actions are used as leverage, to force the victim to act in the desired way. The threat of further action may lead to the cooperation or obedience of the person being coerced.

I had gone through so much heartache and tragedy. I had anxiety and depression and I was using the Family Medical Leave benefit to help me get through the days. The Department did not care and continued to pressure me. Even though I knew that I was a victim of coercion, I was happy to leave to keep my health and sanity.

I contacted the City of Seattle's Retirement Office the very next day. I made an appointment to sign all the papers and found out the earliest I could retire would be January 20th. I was nervous as I signed the papers, but I knew that this career of 25 years was coming to a harsh end.

I thought about a statement that our former Director Herbye White once said. When he first came to work in our Department, he had invited a select few to attend classes that he held in the Board Room, of the 100 Dexter location. He said, "People do business with people."

His words were so true. I knew that there were people that led this Department that I would never want to do "business" with ever again. I signed the retirement papers knowing in just a couple of weeks, I no longer would need to deal with Department leaders that made poor decisions. I would no longer need to deal with Human Resources, as they would tip toe and suck up to those fabricating complaints. I would no longer feel like the "Count of Monte Cristo" or "Sweeny Todd," because of the jealous peers that wanted what I had built. I felt a great burden lifted from me.

HIDING IN THE CAVE

Upon retiring, I really felt lost. For the last 25 years I got up and focused my day for the work I would do for the City of Seattle, Department of Parks and Recreation.

I took pride in that work, but now I felt a great sense of loss. I no longer had to plan for the seasonal special events. I didn't have to worry about getting my reports or brochures in on time. I didn't have to rush off to meetings anymore. I no longer had to get up in the morning with a focused purpose.

The bonus was I didn't have to listen to the ranting of crazy people, while having to demonstrate diplomacy and great restraint. The "crazies" were unreasonable members of the public and staff persons that would make up lies to get whatever they wanted. Some of these people demonstrated deceit and treachery that would have been perfectly suited for television tabloid talk shows.

Having this severe feeling of loss, I remained in the comfort of my "cave." I soon stopped enjoying the activities that made me happy. I was no longer playing basketball, or table tennis.   Trips to the range were a chore.

My comfort zone was the safety of my home and the 500 DVD collection that kept me company.

After the ordeal with the Department my anxiety had left, but the depression remained.

GUARDIAN ANGELS

My usual guardian angels were my sister Susan and brother-in-law Wally. They always had some activity for me to do with them. They were also always the most generous people you could imagine. My sons Jason and Brandon also did a good job keeping me busy too. My nephew Patrick and his girlfriend Vy would find things to do with me, but it usually ended up being Gears (Gears of War 2, a video game for Xbox 360).

Our guardian angels can come in strange forms. My teenagers from Chinatown were Alan Trang, Wil Butler, Sam Almanza and Frances Wu. I would have never thought that these young men would be there to help me and get me out of the house.

I had developed a close relationship with them while I was the Recreation Center Coordinator at the International District/Chinatown Community Center. They had learned to enjoy the activities that I had planned for them and were "regulars" for our special events. They also trained with me during the Teen Kung-Fu Program that I created.

I had an open door policy and these teenagers were often in my office telling me what was the latest in their lives. I was their confidant and role model. Somewhere along the line we became friends.

The boys did great trying to keep me busy and out of my cave. One Friday night at 9:00pm, Sam called me and asked what I was doing. I said that I was just going to relax, stay home watch some movies. He replied, "No you're not. You're coming with us!"

I said, "Thanks, but I'll just stay home." Sam then said, "You have to go with us. We're outside your house. Get dressed, the movie starts pretty soon!" I couldn't refuse and I soon found myself in their car, rushing to a Downtown movie theater.

I sat with them in the front row, something I never do unless I'm very late to a show. There were so many available seats at this 10 p.m showing of The Punisher, but the boys wanted to sit right up front!

The boys were great! They would call me up and we would go out to play table tennis and basketball at Van Asselt Community Center. We would have meals at Burger King, Super Buffet and Kum Kang San Korean BBQ Buffet. We even made it to Snoqualmie Casino's buffet.

Of course we had our Gears of War 2 parties that were extremely fun. The neighbors probably wondered what was going on so late at night, with people coming in and out. What may have looked like illegal activities early in the a.m. were nothing more than food runs for hungry teenagers.

The boys never went back to our community center in Chinatown. They felt once I left there was no reason to go back. They wouldn't go back even though I would go back on occasion and visit the pre-teens and the table tennis players.

One day when we were out playing table tennis together, Sam brought up that he remembered sitting in my office and hearing me say that I would probably work there until I died. We all laughed and they realized things had changed when I was betrayed and treated poorly.

Chac Wu was another unlikely guardian angel. Chac was a table tennis participant at my community center. He loved table tennis and my community center with all the table tennis nights that I had programmed, became his favorite haunt.

I showed up on a few Saturdays and Chac and I would play. After he found out that I really didn't feel comfortable in my old facility, he stated that there was a table tennis league at the Chinese Baptist Church in my neighborhood. He said that many of the players were people that had participated in my community center from Chinatown.

I started playing as a regular in the Chinese Baptist Church table tennis league, and Chac would call me up to get me to play and practice more.

The players at the Chinese Baptist Church table tennis league were always very nice and made me feel welcomed. It was an actual league and it kept records of winning percentages and also factored in attendance. I always enjoyed playing there.

STARTING A NEW STORY

The book I had been working on the past year was "A Kung-Fu Master's Book on Table Tennis." With Susan and Wally's suggestion, I changed the title to "Kung-Fu Table Tennis." Whenever I had some free time while I was taking care of my mother, I was busy writing the table tennis book, or doing story boarding to coordinate photos that would need to be shot for the book. However, I decided to postpone this project and work on a memoir instead. There were many reasons to do this.

My close friend Kregg P.J. Jorgenson had mentioned to me numerous times that I should write a book that all our students should own and study. That way they would know where their martial arts came from and the background that created the style.

I also thought that my personal story was important. The way I was brought up, the time period, the area, all had influences on what I became and who I was.

My martial arts and achievement of to a very high level was unique. Not very many people ever achieve high levels in the martial arts. It is even rarer to create your own style and get to the level that you are respected by the martial arts community. I then also added some of my thoughts and beliefs into my first book.

The first book would become a memoir with my thoughts and teachings. This became a multi-layered project with many angles for the reader to be engaged in. I decided to name the book "A Kung-Fu Master's Journey."

THE UNKNOWN FOCUS POWER OF A.D.D.

I started finding different parts of the project would energize me greatly. I had become mesmerized and spent hours locked on to specific tasks.

The writing was great as I relived the situations in my mind and then wrote them down with my computer.

Inserting the 155 photographs in the book was indeed a great task. I carefully selected the photographs, scanned and cropped them to fit the pages and tried to tie them with specific topic sections.

The process of selecting the pictures was very positive for me. I marveled that I still had these pictures. Some of them were 35 years old. With each picture I selected, I would be brought back in time and relive the moment.

The writing and photograph selection brought out my focus and concentration. This was exactly why children with A.D.D. can stay focused and concentrate on video games, or movies. The interest can spark this high level of concentration and dismiss any distractions.

Numerous times I would be "locked" on to my tasks and would not shut down my computer until 5:00 a.m.

THE DISAPPERANCE OF THE DEMON DEPRESSION

I was so involved with the writing of the book; my focus was entirely on the project.

With the help of my guardian angels, they got me back to my regular activities. I was playing basketball, table tennis, volleyball and teaching Kung-Fu again. My book project kept me busy the rest of the time. From the increased activities, I received increased energy.

I had no time to "hide in my cave," or dwell on bad memories.

I wasn't working the stressful job. This job also was usually worked during "swing shift" hours. This usually created bad eating habits and no time to burn off the late dinner calories.

With my increased activities, reduced stress and not eating so late, I was able to lose weight. In fact I lost 25 pounds from leaving the stressful job and recovering from the depression.

COMPLETION – THE REBIRTH

On October 4, 2008 I finished my story. I was proud of myself for writing the book. It was a huge challenge and I had to bring all the facets together in one single book.

My niece Melissa Chow helped me with the cover creation. I had an idea of what I wanted the cover to look like. She is a very talented graphic artist and it was a simple task for her to create the cover with the dimensions needed by the publisher. She did an outstanding job with the creation.

My cousin Kay Chinn helped create a website to promote the book. He created the website with the color scheme I wanted. He took vintage video clips and integrated them on the website. The website was a success and we received many positive remarks for its look and content.

In addition to the many titles and things that I had achieved, I had now written my first book.

In this process of healing, I had been reborn an author.

IT'S A WONDERFUL LIFE

On December 12, 2009 I had my Launch Party. This event would promote the book and announce to everyone that book was a real, tangible item.

This event started with the planning in October. I had already envisioned that this book launch party would be combined with my previous annual event, the World of Martial Arts; I discussed this event with Doreen Deaver, the coordinator of Jefferson Community Center. She had previously been an employee that I had mentored, my former assistant and always a good friend.

Doreen was great and helpful as always. We set the event for Saturday, December 12th. I had about a month to get all the details nailed down. I chose to keep the event a private affair. I thought that it would be best to do so, to keep the need for security at a minimum.

I got a group of martial arts masters and instructors together for performance on that day. Most of the performers had worked with me for numerous years. I decided to give a couple of new instructors an opportunity to participate.

My martial arts peers have always been eager to help and they did not deviate from this established behavior. I had a full martial arts event programmed and ready to go.

With the monumental nature of this event, I started to call and contact all my old students. This was another huge undertaking as I had not seen some of these students for 25 years or so.

Looking up old phone numbers and calling other students to find numbers to follow up on, was a chore. Facebook was an amazing help. It made contacting those students and friends on Facebook as easy as sending a private message.

I got in touch with an old student Bill Yamamoto on Facebook. He trained with me about 29 years earlier. It was great talking to him and catching up. He then suggested that his Kung-Fu school could possibly do a lion dance. I thought that this would be a nice touch. Traditionally lion dances would be performed to bring good luck to various events. Good luck was something I could use, so I welcomed the lions!

Bill received the approval of his current instructor Sifu Tony Au, that the lion dances would be performed. I was very thankful of Bill's efforts and Sifu Au's generosity.

Now I had the date set up, the 2009 World of Martial Arts ready to go and the guest list was coming together. Now what do we do about refreshments? I discussed this matter with my close friend Kregg P.J. Jorgenson. Since he had written numerous books and had several book launches, I asked him what I should do. He thought simple refreshments should be good enough.

Then I asked my sister Susan and she had a totally different take on the subject of refreshments. From the simple solution, we went to one that would become complex and with super efforts on the part of the cooks and those buying refreshments.

She thought that we should try to make various hors d'oeuvres, and have canned soft drinks and bottled water available. So with three weeks to go, she already had it in her mind where to buy the canned soft drinks and bottled water because they were on sale, I was going to make fried garlic chicken wings, Susan provided two platters of sushi and my niece Melissa made over 100 firecracker shrimp hors d'oeuvres and 15 dozen chocolate chip cookies. My niece Vy made over 100 egg rolls.

It was just before midnight on the evening before the book launch, my car was full of canned soft drinks and I was just making my last minute mass purchase of the bottled water.

At 4:00 a.m. the morning of the event I just got done cutting up the chicken wings and finished marinating them.

I had just finished frying all the garlic chicken wings by 3:00 p.m. The event was going to start in just three hours. I waited to fry all the chicken wings so they would still be somewhat fresh by the beginning of the event.

"Gremlins" somehow stole my newer (10 year old) steel studded wristbands. My Kung-Fu boots were also missing. Damn those Gremlins! I had to find my old steel studded wristbands. These were about 33 years old. For a replacement to my Kung-Fu boots, I decided to wear my black Puma indoor soccer shoes that I had purchased to use for table tennis.

We rushed to the community center and began the setting up of tables and chairs. The food and drinks were displayed beautifully. All the volunteers jumped to their positions.

The weather was bone chilling and I was concerned that the turn out may not be as large as I had hoped. It was December 12th and I started getting concerned that maybe it was too close to Christmas. Maybe most of the guests would be Christmas shopping, or doing other holiday activities.

Much like my favorite Christmas movie "It's a Wonderful Life," people started to come in. I began to feel like that movie's character George Bailey.

I was touched as family and friends continued coming in. From my work with the City of Seattle, there were former co-workers, supervisors, Advisory Council members and participants from the various community centers that I had coordinated.

Students that I hadn't seen in over 25 years appeared. My martial arts friends, former step aerobics instructor, basketball teammates and childhood friends showed up.

They were all here for me. I felt so much joy and happiness for their support and consideration. Their thoughtfulness and caring really made me feel like we were all part of the finale in Frank Capra's 1946 Christmas classic. That scene had a flood of townspeople arrive to help and support George Bailey and the Building and Loan.

At the end of the movie George finds a gift from his guardian angel Clarence. It is a copy of The Adventures of Tom Sawyer with the inscription stating to remember no man is a failure who has friends.

While I didn't receive a book from an angel, I received the attendance of family and friends. That was heartwarming and priceless! That was the greatest gift of all.

I was thankful for my martial arts friends that came out to perform. The impressive opening with the lion dances was performed by the Ying Yong Tong and Vovinam International Lion & Dragon Dance Team.

The martial arts demonstrations that followed were performed by:

Sifu Tony Au - International School of Martial Arts

Master Minh Huynh - Vovinam

Instructor Cecil Longino and the Academia della Spada

Sensei Clifton Jackson - Shito-Ryu Karate

Sifu Blake Emery - Liu He Ba Fa (Water Style)

Sensei Michael Bowser - Shorin-Ryu Karate

Sifu Shawn Miller - Baat Ying Baat Faat Kung-Fu

Sabunim Mike Shintaku - Tang Soo Do

Sensei Joe Pavesi - Chinese Okinawan Karate

Sifu Rusty DeJesus – Tai Chi and Wushu

Sensei Jonathan Bannister - Iaido and Aikiken

The martial arts demonstrations were excellent and very well received.

Approximately 200 people attended this book launch event. The event was a huge success!

This event could not have been realized without the hard work of my volunteers. My son Brandon for his work as the Master of Ceremony; my son Jason for monitoring the facility; my sister Susan and her husband Wally for the numerous refreshments and food; my nieces Melissa Chow and Vy Bui for hors d'oeuvres; my nieces Melissa Chow, Cori Dang, Lynnette Smith and cousin Kathy Chinn for photography; Patrick Yee, Alan Trang, Sam Almanza and Wil Butler for security; Jennifer Habu for reception; Desiree Loper for chair massages and many others.

PHOTO GALLERY
OF THE
DECEMBER 12, 2009 BOOK LAUNCH

Guest checklist and security: Alan Trang, Patrick Yee and Sam Almanza.

My students Bruce Friedman and Sifu Michael Gibson. Bruce's wife Tracy and daughters.

Brother Steven and his wife Stephanie.

Canadian friends Sifu Neil Chan and Sifu Ritchie Chow.

Pulled pork sandwiches, chocolate chip cookies, shrimp hors d'oeuvres, sushi, egg rolls and fried chicken.

Brother-in-law Wally Lee, grand nephew Taylor Dang and sister Susan.

Niece Cassie, sister-in-law Stephanie, nephew Preston and brother Steven.

Ying Yong Tong and Vovinam International Lion & Dragon Dance Team.

Sifu Tony Au demonstrating Chen Style Tai Chi.

Iron Wire Set by the International School of Martial Arts.

Two man weapon set by the International School of Martial Arts.

Hand set by the International School of Martial Arts.

Instructor Cecil Longino and the Academia della Spada.

Academia della Spada European Spear demonstration.

Academia della Spada fencing demonstration.

Sensei Clifton Jackson performing a Shito-Ryu Karate Kata.

Sifu Blake Emery performing Liu He Ba Fa (Water Style).

Sensei Michael Bowser demonstrating Shorin-Ryu Karate Oar.

My student Sifu Shawn Miller performing Baat Ying Baat Faat Yao Kune (Soft Set).

Baat Ying Baat Faat student David Thanphilom performing Dui Kune (Drunken Fist).

Baat Ying Baat Faat student Ricky Thatsanavongsa performing Jong Hop Kune.

Sabunim Mike Shintaku performing a Tang Soo Do form.

Sensei Joe Pavesi demonstrating Chinese Okinawan Karate.

Sifu Rusty DeJesus demonstrating Tai Chi Sword.

The Spear performed by Seattle Wushu.

The Monk's Spade performed by Seattle Wushu.

The Bench performed by Seattle Wushu.

Sensei Jonathan Bannister demonstrating Japanese Target Cutting.

An Iaido Kata.

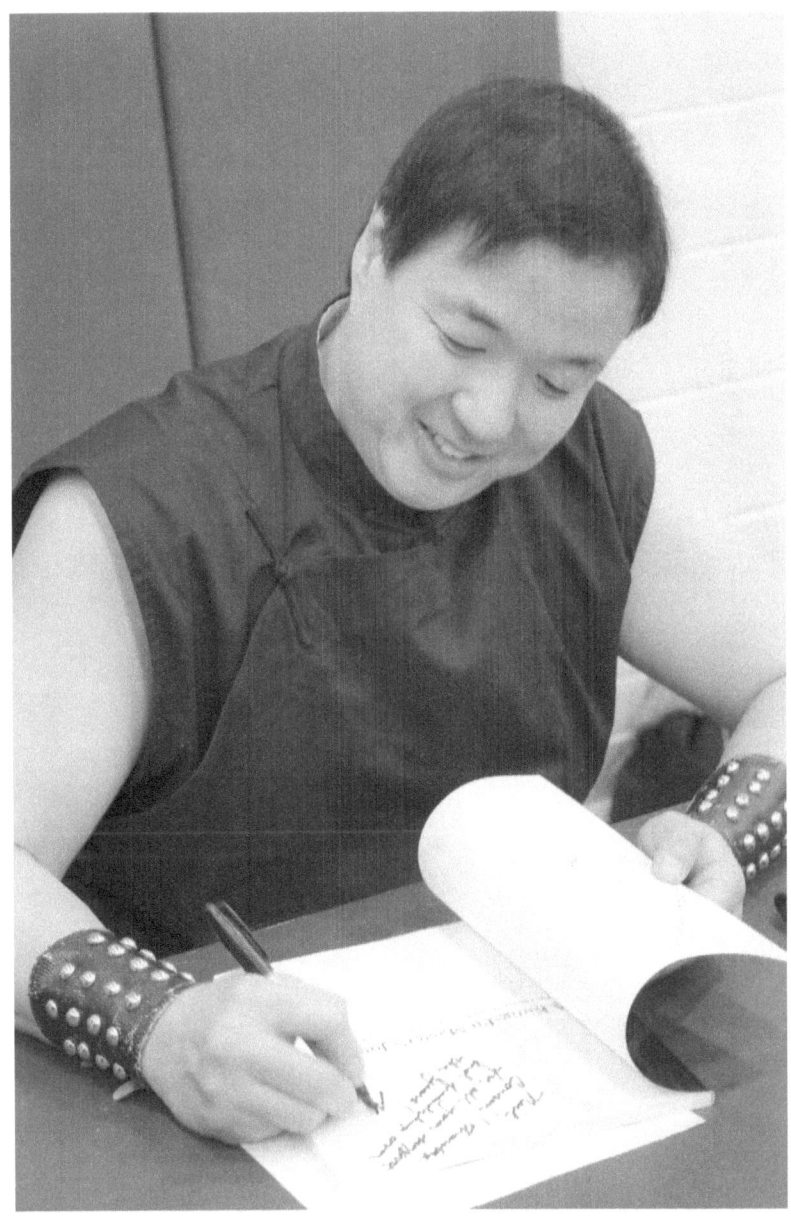

Speaking to Jeff Lewis, my first manager from 1984 at Seattle Parks & Recreation.

Young students Steven Liang, William and Christopher Huie.

Fred and Kathy Young. Basketball, volleyball and family friends.

Cousin Richard Chinn.

My favorite step aerobics instructor Teree Armogeda and classmate Judy Berguis.

Family friends Frederick and Nancy Zee.

Student Ricky Thatsanavongsa with Master Kregg P.J. Jorgenson in the background.

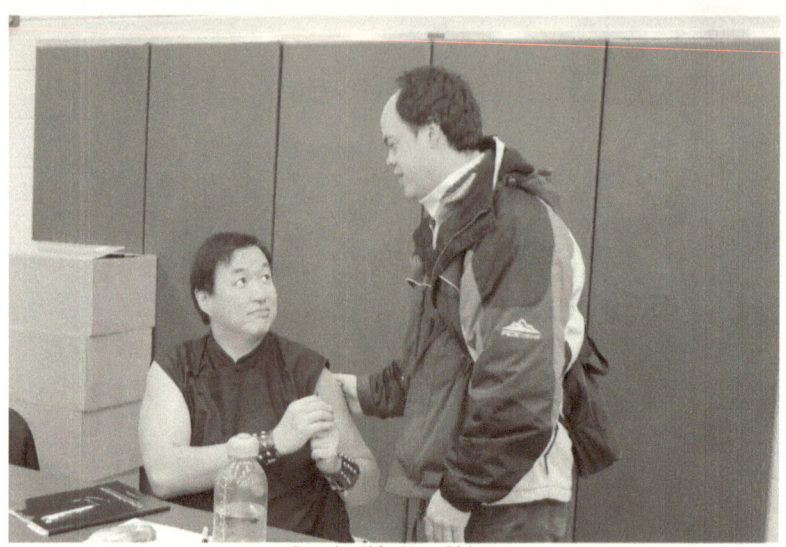

Cousin Sifu Kay Chinn.

My close friend Sifu Neil Chan.

Cousin Kim Chinn, his wife Kathy and children.

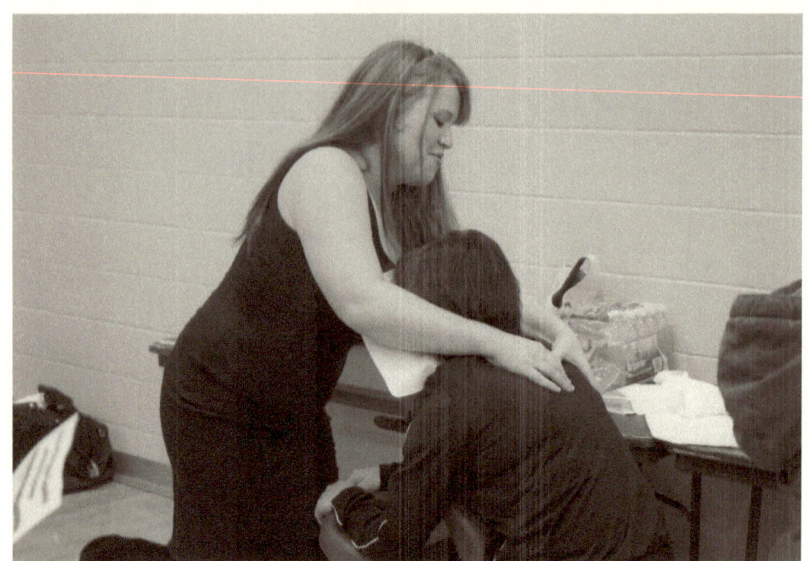

Massage Therapist Desiree Loper performing chair massages.

My son Brandon after he performed as Master of Ceremony.

Congratulatory applauds by the audience.

A few of my Kung-Fu students and friends.

Grand nephew Taylor Dang showing his "cheesy smile."

A few of my Chinatown kids.

Brother-in-law Jim Jorgensen and his wife Shirley.

Niece Lynnette Smith, husband Erick and daughters Cheyenne and Ciara.

My son Jason and his girlfriend Linda Dinh.

Niece Vy Bui and nephew Patrick Yee.

Nieces Cassie Chinn and Melissa Chow.

More family: Toni Perez O'Brien, Jerry Sloan, Carmen Sloan, Cheyenne and Ciara Smith.

Bruce Friedman, my first student from my Bellevue Kung-Fu Club in 1982.

My Seattle Parks and Recreation Manager from 1986, Maureen O'Neill.

Niece Cori Dang, her husband Sun and son Taylor.

My son Brandon and his friend Myranda-Lyn Bell.

A Kung-Fu Master's Journey

The Life and Martial Arts Experiences of an Asian American

By Allen J. Chinn

The front cover of my first book.

Describing 45 years of martial arts experience and the influences that helped shape him, Kung-Fu Grandmaster Allen J. Chinn tells his story.

In a time when little was known about the secret art of Kung-Fu, an eight year old searched to find life's lessons in the Chinese martial arts.

This book gives insight into his experiences as a martial artist, but also describes what it was like growing up as an Asian American in South Seattle's Beacon Hill.

His life experiences and personal thoughts provide the reader an understanding of what makes a 21st century Kung-Fu Grandmaster.

Finally, this book demonstrates that if you desire something enough, you can achieve it. The seemingly impossible can become possible.

ISBN 978-0-557-11572-3

The back cover of my first book.

EPILOGUE

Though I have had tough times with my ex-wives, I do not hold a grudge against them. I realize that I had a part in our failed relationships. My former spouses failed to meet my needs and expectations. I understand that I also failed to meet their needs and expectations.

I believe the hardest thing to do, is have two people with totally different upbringing, life experiences and values, come together.

Add the additional stress of family, friends and finances, and it gets tougher. Factor in incompatible interests and direction and it becomes almost volatile.

I realize that when a relationship doesn't work out, it is far better to walk away and evaluate all factors related to the situation.

There are times that staying together creates greater stress, anxiety, far in excess to what the relationship is worth.

The compromises one makes, can affect everything that we do and who we are. You may be giving in to a situation that you find interesting, but you may be altering what you want in the relationship and the way you behave.

If a relationship does not work out, once the finger pointing ends, it is far better to understand that some things were just not meant to be.

Marriages, like other relationships and partnerships, only work when there are common goals and vision. The compromises are worth the effort, because both parties understand the value of the end rewards.

Commitment to the partnership and the goals can ensure success. Deviate from the agreed goals and instigate individual agendas and the partnership is endangered.

When the stress of being with someone becomes insurmountable, this too becomes a time when we must assess the relationship. Is the relationship still worth the stress and the way you are treated? Do you have your dignity intact? Have you compromised yourself to the point where you are not valued at all?

Marriages, relationships and work are all too similar.

When it is over we must move on. We must rebuild our lives and heal our souls.

Dealing with the death of loved ones is very difficult. We will always cherish the moments we shared with the ones we loved the most. We must accept our loss and celebrate their life that will always live on in our memory.

With all the bad one can receive, no one can foresee other effects that it may have. The grief and loss can become crippling.

18 million Americans suffer from depression and approximately 9 million Americans have major or clinical depression, this is a serious issue.

Since two-thirds of people suffering from depression do not seek the necessary treatment, sometimes family and friends must intervene to assist them.

However, most friends and families if the victims do not understand their great difficulty and struggles at all. As with most afflictions, one can only imagine the difficulties and issues, but it is much graver for the people that go through it. The cure for depression is not quick, or simple.

Like George Bailey in "Its a Wonderful Life," when great stress and sadness occurs, one may question if the world might be better off without them. This is where thoughts of suicide could occur.

According to the Center for Disease Control in 2007, suicide was the tenth leading cause of death in the U.S., accounting for 34,598 deaths. An estimated 11 attempted suicides occur per every suicide death.

Though not all depression victims consider suicide, this is still a valid concern.

Those guardian angels in our lives can really help us through the tough times. Sometimes we may need professional help. We just need to understand that this option is acceptable and we shouldn't hesitate if it helps us deal with issues that can cripple us.

When our lives have been burned to the ground, we can be reborn. What we do to recreate ourselves, or relearn to be ourselves and flourish, is something we can and must do.

Be happy, reborn to your true self and thrive.

www.ingramcontent.com/pod-product-compliance
Lightning Source LLC
Chambersburg PA
CBHW030402290526
45785CB00004B/1872